THE CREATIVE BOOK OF

Flower
Arranging

THE CREATIVE BOOK OF

Flower Arranging

Created by Jan Hall

a Salamander book

Published by Salamander Books Limited
LONDON • NEW YORK

Published by Salamander Books Ltd.,
52 Bedford Row,
London WC1R 4LR,
England.

©Salamander Books Ltd. 1987
ISBN 0 86101 290 9

Distributed by Hodder and Stoughton Services,
PO Box 6, Mill Road, Dunton Green,
Sevenoaks, Kent TN13 2XX.

CREDITS

Floral designs by: Jan Hall

Authors: Introduction by Angela Vokolek;
step-by-step instructions by Coral Walker

Editor-in-chief: Jilly Glassborow

Designer: Barry Savage

Photographer: Steve Tanner

Typeset by: The Old Mill, London

Colour separation by: Fotographics Ltd, London – Hong Kong

Printed in Belgium by: Proost International Book Production

CONTENTS

Introduction	7
Buying Flowers	8
Conditioning	10
Equipment	14
Floral Design	16
Flower Arrangements	18
Conditioning Chart	124
Index	126

INTRODUCTION

This delightful book takes a fresh, new look at flower arranging, breaking away from more formal designs to create an altogether freer effect. There are, of course, the more classical designs in conventional vases but, in the main, the majority of displays are based upon using unusual and sometimes quite outrageous containers found in all rooms of the home. Containers like fancy paper or plastic bags, toy trucks, goldfish bowls, pineapples and even gumboots! No longer do you need lovely vases to create stimulating and exotic arrangements.

Apart from step-by-step instructions on how to create the many beautiful arrangements featured, there is also essential information on the buying of flowers, how to condition and re-condition them, which types of foliage to grow at home, the basic equipment and mechanics of flower arranging, plus the importance of design and colour in creating a well-balanced floral display.

Throughout the book, the plants have been given their most commonly used name — which is often the Latin name — for example, gypsophilia rather than baby's breath, ivy rather than *Hedera*. For easy reference, however, a full list of scientific conversions (common name to Latin name) appears at the end of the book on page 126.

——FLOWER ARRANGING——

Flower arranging dates back to the ancient Egyptians who used plant material for decorative purposes as long ago as 2,500 BC. Since then other cultures and nations have come and gone, yet the pleasure of decorating our homes with flowers remains. During this century flower arranging has become even more popular and most people have some plant or floral arrangement in their hall or living rooms.

Flower arranging need not be expensive, especially if you have a garden. As well as background information on how best to prolong the flowers and plants that you display, we have given step-by-step instructions to specific arrangements which can readily be adapted to the availability of flowers and the different types of containers you may have in your home.

——BUYING FLOWERS——

For many people without a garden, a florist's shop, supermarket or market flower stall is the main source of flowers. Although this can be more expensive than picking blooms from your own garden, you can ensure you get the very best for your money by observing the following guidelines.

Generally, all purchased flowers will need refreshing when they reach your home. Re-cut their stems and give them a long drink for a few hours before transferring them to shallow water and a warm room. Most florists condition flowers before they are sold, so you should only consider re-conditioning them if they begin to wilt (see page 27).

In the spring and summer there will be generally more choice of flowers available. The flowers will probably also be less expensive than in the winter, when most of the florist's stock will either have been imported or grown in hot-house conditions.

Spray chrysanthemums are a good buy all year round as they should last for up to three weeks. During the summer months it is better to buy the outdoor bunch chrysanthemums rather than the more costly forced sprays. When buying these, always look for tight, firm centres and if they are single varieties ensure the centres are firm and yellow as opposed to fluffy and golden.

Spray carnations are another good purchase as they are also good survivors. Buy when they are firm and not fully opened; all the buds should open eventually.

Gladioli are best bought during the summer months, their natural season. Forced, hot-house gladioli can very often not open due to being cut too early.

Copper, porcelain, wood, terracotta, plain or coloured glass; traditional, unconventional, modern or antique — all can enhance the natural beauty of flowers.

Orchids are excellent value for money. Both *Dendrobium* and *Cymbidium* orchids can last for as long as two months. Take care when purchasing these flowers though, and avoid any fully-opened sprays or brown-edged petals.

Stocks are very short-lived, although they are usually inexpensive and emit a beautiful perfume. Their stems quickly become soft and smelly in water, so bear this in mind when arranging.

Freesias — with their powerful fragrance — can live for well over a week if bought when only the first flower is showing, the rest in bud.

All spring bulb flowers should be purchased in bud as their life is short once fully opened.

Roses are best purchased in the summer months when they are in season. In the winter they tend to be expensive and of an inferior quality; consequently they are likely to die quite quickly without even opening fully.

Most florists' flowers are sold in peak condition, but do seek out a shop where the flowers look healthy and well presented. Flowers bought from a market stall may not have been conditioned and although perhaps less expensive will need extra attention when you return home. Wherever you buy flowers the golden rule is to look for good, crisp foliage, strong straight stems and tight, firm flower buds.

CONDITIONING

Most living things respond to a little care and attention, and plants are no exception. To prolong the life of cut flowers and foliage you need to condition them. Generally, flowers bought from a florist will have been conditioned before they are sold, so they will only need their stems re-cut and a long, cool drink.

It is best to pick flowers from the garden in the early evening when transpiration (water loss) is low and the plant is well charged with 'food' after photosynthesizing all day. Cut the stems at an angle as this allows a larger area to absorb the water. Place immediately into a bucket of tepid water and leave for several hours, even overnight if possible, as this will give the plants time to fully charge up with moisture. Keep in a cool, shady place in summer and a frost-free area in winter. If the place or water is too warm some of the buds may begin to open prematurely. You must also ensure that all plant material is kept away from draughts as these cause dehydration.

Some flowers naturally last longer than others, but all can be prolonged with care. Adding preservatives to the water will help to prolong the life of a display. These can be purchased from a florist or, alternatively, you can simply add a spoonful of sugar, an aspirin tablet or even a dash of lemonade to the water — all work equally well. Before beginning a display, you should also ensure your container is clean as this will help to reduce the growth of stem-clogging bacteria.

All plants take in water through their stems and these vary considerably in structure. Chrysanthemums, stocks and roses have soft, woody stems and such plants need their stem ends crushed lightly with a hammer so that the inner, absorbing, plant tissue is reached. Alternatively, a couple of upward slits can be made in the base of the stem with a sharp knife. Forsythia, rhododendron, lilac and *Prunus*

Condition woody stems by making two upward slits with a sharp knife.

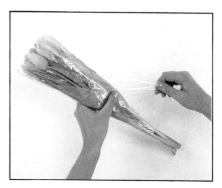

Straighten and strengthen tulips by wrapping them in non-absorbent paper.

have hard, woody stems. These will need the outside bark scraped off at the base of the stem before crushing or splitting to achieve maximum water absorption.

Soft-stemmed flowers include most spring bulb flowers such as iris, tulips and freesia. These will absorb water quickly and easily so place them in shallow water at first, as deep water may encourage them to open too rapidly. (While conditioning tulips, wrap them in stiff, non absorbent paper for a couple of hours to help them straighten before arranging.) Gladioli — with their strong stems — also need shallow water, but to help all the flowers to open, remove the last few small buds from the tip of the stem to encourage the lower ones to bloom.

Some plants have hollow stems and taller varieties, such as delphinium and the larger headed dahlias, require some help to ensure that the water reaches the top of the stem and into the flower head. To do this, turn the bloom upside down, fill up the stem with cold water and plug it with a little cotton wool.

Short-lived flowering shrubs such as lilac, *Viburnum* and mock orange blossom need as much water as possible to reach the flower heads. This can be achieved by stripping off the leaves.

Some flowers are best conditioned through their heads first, rather than their stems. Violets are one such example. Place the heads into tepid water for 30 minutes and then, turning the plants upside down, put the stems into cool, shallow water.

Some plants, such as *Euphorbia* and poppies, emit a milky substance from the cut stem which can form a seal, thus preventing water absorption. To stop this, sear the end of the stem by holding it over a flame until it goes black. (This milky substance can also cause irritation to the skin and should be washed off immediately.)

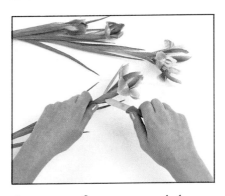

Open out iris flowers prematurely by slicing through sepals with a knife.

Encourage gladioli to open fully by removing last few small buds.

RE-CONDITIONING

Generally speaking, it is best to change the water in a display regularly, though some manufacturers of preservatives may recommend that this is not necessary when using their product. Florists' foam in particular needs regular watering to prevent it from drying out; if it does begin to dry out it will cause the flowers to droop. Some flowers, however, may begin to droop even though they have recently been conditioned and are not short of water. In this case the flowers need to be re-conditioned. Cut off about 2.5cm (1in) from the end of the stems and place them into hot shallow water for ten minutes, protecting the flower heads from the steam with a layer of tissue or soft paper. Then remove the flowers and place them into deep, cool water, leaving them for at least one hour before rearranging them.

FOLIAGE CONDITIONING

A variety of long-lasting foliage is usually obtainable from a florist. Alternatively, there are many attractive varieties that can easily be grown in the garden (see opposite).

Prolong the life of woody-stemmed foliage such as eucalpytus, rhododendron, camellia, box *(Buxus sempervirens), Ruscus, Cupressus, Pittosporum,* and beech by hammering or slitting their stems before giving them a long drink of water. Ivy and heather like to be totally immersed into deep, cool water for an hour before arranging. Hydrangea heads also like this treatment but for only half the time.

Remember that any foliage placed under the water level in an arrangement will decay, so always strip away any leaves that might otherwise fall beneath the surface of the water.

Sear cut stems by holding over a flame until the end goes black.

Help woody stems to absorb water by crushing the ends with a hammer.

Shrubs to Grow at Home

Have an abundant supply of foliage for floral displays by growing your own. Most of these shrubs can be grown in pots or urns on balconies or patios.

Buxus sempervirens (box) Good strong small dark green leaves which will last for weeks when cut and placed in water.

Aucuba japonica (spotted laurel) Large yellow-green spotted leaves that grow easily in a pot and last well in water.

Camellia
A long lasting foliage which has thick glossy leaves and pretty flowers like small roses.

Cupressocyparis (leyland cypress) A fast growing conifer with feathery green sprays which last well when cut.

Cytisus scoparius (broom) Long, narrow sprays which form small pea-shaped flowers in late spring.

Choisya ternata (Mexican orange blossom) A glossy evergreen with sweetly-scented blooms in late spring.

Euonymus europaeus (spindle tree) A hardy small leaf shrub with many varieties and colours.

Forsythia
Best used in spring when the golden flowers are in bloom.

Gaultheria shallon
Large leathery green rounded leaves; very long lasting.

Hebe
A strong and hardy flowering shrub which boasts 100 species. It lasts well in water when cut.

Mahonia aquifolium (Oregon grape) A shrub with holly-like leaves and fruits that resemble grapes.

Skimmia japonica
A hardy shrub with small thick leaves and white flowers.

EQUIPMENT

A few basic pieces of equipment are necessary before you begin arranging any floral display. These include a good strong pair of florist's scissors or secateurs, a small watering can with a long spout to re-water the arrangement, and a sharp knife for cutting tough stems or stripping away foliage.

Apart from the equipment, actual supports - or mechanics - may also be necessary to arrange the display. Basically, the mechanics are florists' foam, wire mesh or netting, pin-holders and any weighty objects such as marbles, pebbles, shells and so on.

FLORISTS' FOAM
Foam is the most popular mechanic of the florist. It is a specially manufactured substance which readily absorbs water and supports any stems inserted into it, providing they are not too heavy. It can be bought in bricks or rounds of various sizes and, for a fresh arrangement, simply needs soaking in cold water before using. Never let an arrangement in foam dry out as it will not take up water again. Foam meant for fresh displays can be kept moist and sealed in an airtight plastic bag when not used. Foam's only disadvantage is that it tends to break up if the stems are too heavy or if it is over soaked or over used. A form of florists' foam is also available for dried arrangements.

WIRE MESH
Wire mesh is best for heavy stems and more random displays. Buy 5cm (2in) mesh, preferably plastic coated, to avoid scratching the inside of your containers. Crumple the mesh and shape it into the container ensuring the holes formed are of an adequate size to receive and support the foliage and flower stems. Alternatively, wrap it around some florists' foam to provide extra support. Important points to remember when using wire mesh are not to crush it too tightly so that it is impossible to insert the stems, and also to leave the mesh more open in the centre where most of the stems will converge.

PIN-HOLDERS
A pin-holder is a heavy metal base studded with a large number of small, upright pins onto which the stems are impaled. A 7.5cm (3in) diameter pin-holder is probably the most useful size for the novice flower arranger. This form of mechanic is particularly useful when designing an arrangement using a limited number of flowers in a shallow container. When introducing the stems to the pin-holder place them vertically and ease them gently to the required angle. Woody

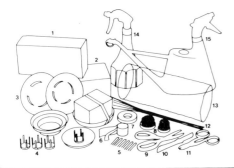

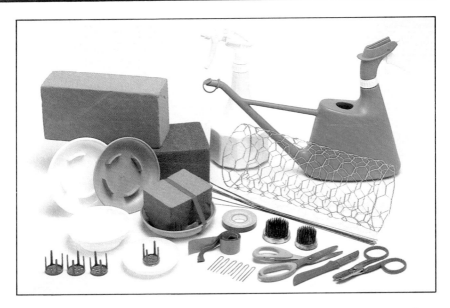

stems should be split upwards from the base to help secure them to the pins. Light-weight plastic pin-holders are small devices used for securing florists' foam and are often used in conjunction with a fixative to secure the foam to the base of a container.

MARBLES AND PEBBLES

All the above mechanics require to be hidden by the flowers, foliage or the container itself. However, pretty translucent marbles or attractively coloured pebbles provide a form of support which can look particularly impressive when seen through a striking glass container. The stems are inserted into the objects which shift slightly as the arrangement progresses; such mechanics are not therefore ideal for a more regimental display. Other objects, such as shells, can also provide an attractive support for arrangements.

OTHER AIDS

Purpose-designed plastic saucers are useful bases on which to tape florists' foam — dry or soaked — before placing into a container. Apart from tape, U-pins and wire are alternatives for fixing foam to bases, particularly unusual types such as driftwood. Wire is also handy for designs which require some adjustment of the container, for example when propping open the lid of a basket. Plastic-coated wire can support fragile or brittle stems but should be used sparingly as it can give an unnatural appearance to the plants.

FLORAL DESIGN

The best flowers and foliage can look positively 'wrong' simply because no thought has gone into the design of the display. Generally, design means considering three basic principles before you begin: outline and form; harmony (colour and setting); and balance and scale.

The shape of an arrangement depends largely on the flowers and foliage you are using, e.g. tall stems, round full blooms etc. Tall flowers or foliage usually establish the height or outline of a display, while bold flowers or full blooms very often form the focal point, or the centre, of an arrangement. Other flowers and foliage are used to fill in the outline, and contrasting colours or textures can be recessed into the arrangement to give depth. The angle from which the arrangement is to be seen will also affect the shape of the finished display to some extent. Consider whether the display will be seen face on, or from all sides. If the arrangement is to serve as a dinner party centrepiece it should be low-lying.

Harmony is really self explanatory. Look at the colours; do they contrast? Or are they toning and from the same area of the colour spectrum (see colour wheel opposite)? In what or on what is the display being set? And where is it going to be seen? Quite often the setting of any display, i.e. coffee table, entrance lobby, guest bedroom or wherever, is of vital importance. A small 'posy' in a delicate container would be utterly lost in a large room. So think of the position of the display, the lighting of the room and so forth.

Above all, a display should be well balanced — looking neither top heavy nor lopsided. It can be either a traditional symmetrical design, or a more free-flowing and random one. Before you start an arrangement, decide on the type of display you wish to create, whether it is to be symmetrical or asymmetrical, triangular or semi-circular. Alternatively,

Right: Flowers and foliage placed equally on each side of an arrangement form a symmetrical display.

Symmetrical

Centre: Long stems have been used to create a strong diagonal line running through this attractive asymmetrical arrangement.

Far right: Flowers are clustered into groups in a continental fashion in this triangular arrangement.

Yellow

Yellow-green

Yellow-orange

Green

Orange

Blue

Orange-red

Blue-violet

Red

Violet

Red-violet

This wheel is a guide to colour harmony. Warm colours (red, yellow, orange) sit on one side of the wheel, the cool colours (blue, violet, green) on the other. Complementary colours are those opposite each other on the wheel.

you may decide upon a linear design (as on page 103) or a lazy-S (Hogarth) design (see page 90). Think ahead about how the flowers will be positioned to best balance each other and avoid putting large blooms above smaller, delicate stems — this tends to make the arrangement look top heavy.

Another clever way to achieve a pleasing result is to arrange the flowers in groups — a popular continental style — to form an asymmetrical triangle (see below).

Asymmetrical

Continental

A silver rose bowl is designed to show off roses to their best advantage as this rich display of full blown yellow roses and golden freesias demonstrates. Fill the bowl with water. Then cut short the stems of the cream spider chrysanthemums (to around 5cm, 2in) and pack into the bowl's wire mesh centre — these will give depth to the final arrangement.

Finally, place *Leucodendron* and freesia buds among the display, ensuring the stems are slightly longer than those of the other flowers; these will provide a stark contrast to the gold and silver. For a short period of time, such as during a dinner party, a full blown rose at the foot of the bowl will complete the picture, though, out of the water, the bloom's lifespan will be limited.

Place yellow roses in between the chrysanthemums, keeping the stems slightly longer. Next, intersperse the arrangement with a few freesias.

The bold yellows and reds of the flowers offset the deep blue glass of this attractive 1930s bowl. Crushed wire mesh is the best medium for this type of shallow bowl as it keeps the flowers from sagging.

Fill mesh with variegated *Pittosporum*, a bushy foliage which maintains its fullness even when cut short. Stems of gypsophilia (also known as baby's breath in the United States) are added next, spread across the arrangement.

The three main stems of yellow lily, straddling the length of the vase, form the focal point. Intersperse the whole display with holly (known more specifically as English holly in the United States) berries, retaining the longer twigs for contrast and balance.

This stunning display of rich pinks and purples beautifully complements the handsome lilac-glazed vase. Using a tall vase, such as this, warrants a lofty arrangement. Begin by putting some chunks of soaked florists' foam into the vase and creating the outline with long stems of eucalyptus. Strengthen the outline with four or five deep pink gladioli.

Cut dark purple spray chrysanthemums to varying lengths and form a 'central column' through the middle of the display, leaving one small flower head to hang gently down over the rim of the vase. Follow this line with four deep pink roses. Finally, use delicate sprays of *Dendrobium* orchids to strengthen the outline, reserving one or two to gently curve downwards.

A deep blue vase in art nouveau style is cleverly contrasted by an exquisite arrangement of gentle colours and contours. Put only water into the vase; the vase's tight neck will support the display. Position several sprays of sprengeri fern, curving one piece so that it sweeps down in front of the vase. Then two long stems and one shorter one of pale creamy-pink alstroemeria.

Create a central column using white lilac; this will give depth to the arrangement. Then take stems of pink daisy chrysanthemums in graduating lengths and place throughout the display.

The frosty pink glass of this art deco vase is reflected in the flowers of the display. Squash up a piece of wire mesh and squeeze into the bottom of the vase: the mesh will be masked by the frosted glass.

Add long stems of pink broom to form the curving outline. Then fill in the outline with pink miniature roses.

Pink gerbera form the focal point. Place one above the other to the front of the arrangement, with three more looking out from the sides. Finally, fill in the gaps with pinks, recessing some of the flowers as shown to create depth in the arrangement.

The beauty of these 'triangular'-shaped vases is that they can be used to create an attractive 'sweeping fan' effect. Place marbles in the vase to stabilize the arrangement before adding water. Then begin the outline with yellow broom, curving the pieces out from the vase.

Arrange the remaining flowers in groups. First, the yellow lilies, keeping the flowers at differing heights to obtain maximum focal effect; next the white chrysanthemums on the opposite side.

Fill in the outline with stems of *Oncidium ornithorhynchum* orchids and a spray of forsythia.

Simplicity itself, this modern design relies on straight lines and bold colours to create a striking effect. Carefully fill an oblong glass vase with marbles, then cover with water.

Cut three stems of amaryllis — two of similar length and one slighty longer — and push into the marbles. The hollow amaryllis stems will curl when placed into water, so the marbles are excellent for holding them in position.

Position the two shorter stems together on one side of the vase, the other longer one on the opposite side.

This oblong glass vase displays all the individual varieties of flowers prominently. Fill the vase with marbles then with water. Position the purple iris first, taking stems of similar length and placing them so that they lean on one side of the vase.

Because the marbles shift slightly as you insert the stems, it is usually easier to work from one side of the vase to the other. So next take the grey *Kochia* (summer cypress) foliage and place alongside the irises to the back of the vase. In front of the *Kochia* group some pink nerines.

Position several mid-blue scabious (known as pincushion flowers in the United States) of varying length next, and finally, four or five bright pink hyacinths to complete the arrangement.

A mass of flowers in harmonizing blues, lilacs, purples and white combine to create a splendid arrangement, ideal for an entrance hall or lobby. Pack soaked florists' foam into the neck of a plain glazed pot. Begin with the tallest flowers first: purple statice and blue dyed yarrow. Work in descending stages so that each flower is 'sitting' on another.

Working gradually downwards, intermix the statice and yarrow with white daisy chrysanthemums, delphniums and *Euphorbia marginata*, having seared this latter plant first (see page 11). Keep some of the upper leaves on the stems of the flowers as these give depth to the display. To finish, follow through the shape of the arrangement with blue-dyed carnations.

Brighten up a potted plant with a few added flowers. Insert several little phials — or any small, slim containers — of water into the soil of the plant. Place them evenly around the pot and fill with long stems of mimosa so that the flowers occupy the spaces between the leaves. Mimosa works very well with this dumb cane, picking up the yellow-green of the variegated leaves.

Complete the effect by placing the pot into a pottery plant holder. This display should last well, but remember to water the phials regularly. An equally pleasing effect can be achieved using just one or two small containers of water, placed at the back or side of the display, and filled with a small group of flowers.

This traditionally shaped vase looks particularly attractive with a bright and bold symmetrical arrangement. The blues reflect the vase while the pink of the gerbera is a perfect complement and forms the focal point of the display. Fill the vase with water and build up the outline using eucalyptus and September flowers (a form of aster). Curve the eucalyptus down towards the base of the display, and position the feathery September flowers upright at the back.

Add to the outline by inserting a few stems of pink gladioli, one shorter than the others. (Tip: nip out the 'plait' at the end of the gladiola stem before arranging as this encourages the buds to open and makes the display last longer.)

Fill in the outline with white and blue delphiniums. Then add the focal flowers by positioning five or six stems of gerbera at the front of the arrangement. Recess a few white spray chrysanthemums and finish off with two or three stems of bells of Ireland to contrast with the soft texture of the other flowers.

This stunning display resembles a rather spectacular hat and is easily created using a plain round cake tin. Tape a piece of soaked florists' foam on to a saucer and place inside the tin. Create the outline with variegated and ordinary *Ruscus* and white snapdragons, using the latter to form a gentle diagonal line.

The main focal flowers are deep red chrysanthemums — graduate their height so they completely fill the centre of the display. To finish the arrangement take six or seven stems of red *Arachnis* (scorpion) orchids and position them throughout the display, strengthening and extending the outline.

A shallow ovenware dish forms the base for this arrangement of fiery chrysanthemums, carnations and capsicums (also known as Christmas pepper in the United States). Place soaked florists' foam into the dish and cover with *Viburnum tinus* allowing the stems to escape over the sides of the dish.

To create the focal point of the arrangement, take six full blooming orange carnations and arrange them uniformly across the outline.

Fill in the outline with greenish white spray chrysanthemums. Their colour provides a dramatic contrast to the orange carnations, and their flame-shaped petals aptly fit the theme of the arrangement. Complete the display with capsicums, taking them through and along the length of the arrangement.

The kitchen is often the first place to look for useful containers. Pretty aluminium cases such as these are shiny and create attractive highlights. Place a piece of soaked florists' foam into the case. Then add long stems of *Viburnum tinus* to create the outline.

Spray some longer stems of eucalyptus with silver paint and, when they are dry, slot them in among the *Viburnum*. Paint-sprayed dried foliage is an excellent addition to any arrangement especially when using a metallic base or container.

Form the focal point of the display, and help to fill in the outline, using dark red spray carnations — both buds and full flowers. For depth, recess some dark red *Viburnum* buds. A little water and a few flowers in the mini cases complete the display.

A stoneware pestle and mortar forms an unusual and attractive setting for an arrangement, the soft neutral colours complemented by the grey-green foliage and strikingly contrasted by the rich pinks and purples. To begin, tape soaked florists' foam to a small dish which will fit inside the mortar.

Build up the outline of the arrangement with the grey succulent foliage *Kochia* (summer cypress) — this will give depth to the final display. Add a few blue-purple forget-me-nots, placing them among the foliage.

Position dark pink spray chrysanthemums to form the focal point of the arrangement and to help fill in the outline. Finally add some stems of striking *Mallalika* foliage. To create an asymmetrical effect place the *Mallalika* so that it flows diagonally (as shown here). Follow this line with some long stems of chrysanthemum buds.

Create a pretty country picture with a wicker bread basket and a selection of colourful garden flowers. Tape a piece of soaked florists' foam into a small saucer and place in the basket. Cover the foam with *Viburnum tinus* foliage, then take long, feathery stems of yellow broom and position so that a 'spidery' effect is formed.

Add bolder yellow flowers in the form of clumps of forsythia, cut quite short and rising up from the centre and towards the foreground of the display.

Create the focal point using rust-coloured daisy chrysanthemums to form a dome shape, and fill in any gaps with a few sprays of golden freesias.

This low circular arrangement could serve well as a centrepiece on a large round table. Tape soaked florists' foam to a dinner plate and place in the basket. Cover the foam with partly-sprayed gold hydrangea heads. Then position six or seven open lilies and two or three buds amidst the hydrangea, keeping the stems short so that they sit low.

Add deep rust spray chrysanthemums — cut even shorter — to nestle close in behind the lilies, giving depth. Contrast these with paler coppery spider chrysanthemums, inserting them in any gaps.

To finish, dot longer stems of brown preserved eucalyptus and pieces of coral sparingly throughout the arrangement. These give contrast both in colour and texture.

Brilliant scarlet anemones dominate this lovely display which nestles in an old-fashioned enamelled colander. Tape a piece of soaked florists' foam to a saucer and secure it in the colander with some florists' fixative. Then use feathery marguerite foliage to cover the foam and form the base and outline for the flowers.

The final effect is one of a 'ball' of flowers sitting on a stand. This rounded effect is created with the red anemone flowers which should be positioned with their faces looking up and out from the display.

Now the outline has been created with the flowers and foliage, fill in the gaps with sprays of pretty September flowers (a form of aster). These contrast well in both texture and colour, and enhance the focal flowers — the anemones.

This is a rather enterprising use for an ordinary metal sieve, and one which works surprisingly well with wintery flowers and foliage. Use a piece of soaked florists' foam wrapped completely in cling film (plastic wrap) as the base for the sieve. Adhere the sieve to the foam with some wire or pins. Next secure another soaked brick of foam inside the sieve.

Cover the foam with flowering *Viburnum tinus,* creating both a solid base for the display and a strong diagonal line. This will give the eye a firm visual route to follow.

Take the very palest of pink spray chrysanthemums, cutting the individual flowers from the sprays rather than using the main stem. Position a few full flowers in the centre of the display to form the focal point. Several longer stems of chrysanthemum buds and flowers can then be interspersed throughout the outline.

opular in Japan, displays such as this are designed to look like miniature gardens. Here, a round pie dish has been used to form the shallow base. Begin by putting slices of soaked florists' foam of varying thickness into the bottom of the dish and cover with bun moss.

Then take two or three different types of foliage in graduating heights (shown here is *Leucodendron*) and position among the moss mounds.

Cluster some alstroemeria to the foreground, keeping them low and 'bushy'. Place a little *Viburnum tinus* at each side of the alstroemeria. Cut down a gladiola and insert at an angle so that it sits like a ship's masthead on the rim of the dish. Complete with a few miniature carnations, in the same colour as the gladiola, rising up and meeting the foliage behind.

Here, an oblong pie dish forms the base of another low and oriental-style arrangement, in which flowers and foliage are used to create a miniature garden. Put left over chunks of soaked florists' foam into a pie dish and cover with bun moss.

Insert a little *Leucodendron* foliage and two or three sprays of forsythia to serve as trees and bushes.

Then add a small cluster of miniature carnations and *Viburnum tinus* flowers to the foreground, serving as the flowers of the garden and forming the focal point of the display.

A russet-coloured terracotta chicken brick or casserole provides a perfect setting for an orange and golden arrangement. Place a large piece of soaked florists' foam into the 'dish' of the chicken brick. Begin the display with feathery *Mallalika* foliage, fanning it out at the back to establish the height and positioning several stems forward to give a base for the flowers.

Recess a few pale yellow spidery chrysanthemums. Now take several longer stems, place two or three to the right of the arrangement and position two slightly shorter ones on the left, so that they sit on the rim of the dish. Add several rust-coloured daisy chrysanthemums, spreading them throughout the display.

 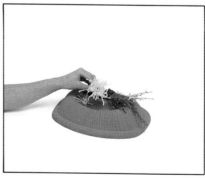

Fill out the arrangement with deep orange carnations, bringing one slightly forward over the rim of the dish. Balance this with a corresponding tall carnation at the back. Complete the display with long stems of yellow broom, following the outline of the *Mallalika.*

Add some water to the lid of the chicken brick and position a few stems of foliage and a flower or two. Keep the plants lying low so that they enhance, and do not detract, from the main display.

. . . and all things nice! An unused spice rack makes a promising wall vase. Use only a few of the jars available, otherwise the arrangement will look too crowded. Fill the jars with water and begin from the left with a small cluster of deep purple anemones and pink roses. Use about six flowers in all. Then move on to another jar.

In a second jar place another dark purple anemone and some pale pink alstroemeria. Finally, create a tall arrangement at the end with dark pink roses, white stock and matching pink tulips. The stock is quite a tall flower, so establish the height with this before cutting any of the other flower stems too short.

A fondue sitting on a burner acts rather like a vase on a pedestal, with both the flowers and the container easily visible — as the bright orange of the pan is an integral part of the display this is quite important. First, put a large piece of soaked florists' foam into the pan. Then form the outline with feathery foliage such as *Mallalika*.

Fill in the centre of the display with peach coloured spray chrysanthemums. Take longer stems of dark red *Arachnis* (scorpion) orchids and place them sparingly throughout the arrangement, following and strengthening the basic outline.

Five red roses form the focal point and balance the colour of the display. Keep four roses of much the same height in the centre, with one longer stem rising from the back and curving gently outwards.

This is a good way of using up broken flower heads or those flowers which could last a few days longer if cut short. Stick double-sided tape around the outside edge of a sponge ring mould. Adhere pleated green cellophane to this and secure with a little more sticky tape. This creates an attractive trim and is an alternative to foliage.

Insert chunks of soaked florists' foam into the ring, placing slightly thicker pieces at the back. Working around the ring insert short stems of daisy chrysanthemums to complete the circle.

Throughout the chrysanthemums dot blue-dyed yarrow and some little gold-sprayed cones on wires. Three white candles complete the garland. (The non-drip variety are best for a floral arrangement.)

With its contrasting colours and textures, this attractive display is a mass of flowers, foliage and wood. Two cast iron skillets, set with soaked florists' foam, form the basis of the display. Begin with the larger skillet, covering the foam with *Choisya ternata* foliage to create an outline. Slot several orange tulips among the outline, curving one tulip down beyond the pan handle.

Recess some stems of peach coloured *Euphorbia fulgens* in among the tulips and foliage, reserving two or three stems to rise up at the side and back of the display. (Remember to sear the *Euphorbia* first, see page 11).

The smaller skillet contains a very simple arrangement of Portuguese laurel leaves and white lilies. Use just three lilies, cutting them short so that they nestle in the skillet among the foliage.

An obsolete electric copper
kettle, burnished and glowing,
makes an attractive and practical
container for flowers. Remove the
lid, which can be used as an
accessory to the arrangement, and
place a piece of soaked florists' foam
into the kettle.

Take just three pieces of eucalyptus
and arrange to create a 'triangle'
which sweeps down diagonally to
the base of the kettle. Already the
dark green-brown foliage and the red
eucalyptus flowers are creating an
attractive effect.

Next, recess some dark rust
chrysanthemums among the foliage,
allowing a few longer stems to
protrude. Finally, use three or four
orange lilies (which have been
previously cut on the slant, and
given a long drink in cold water) to
add colour and to form the focal
point, placing their 'faces' to look
forward from the centre of the
arrangement.

The glow of polished copper provides a perfect setting for this contrasting warm auburn and pale yellow arrangement. Cut and soak half a block of florists' foam and place it in the base of a saucepan. Then form the outline using *Leucodendron*. The larger stem seen here — *L. brunia* — has an interesting texture and helps create depth in the arrangement.

Using a combination of buds and fully opened flowers, take the yellow carnations and arrange them at random around and among the *Leucodendron*.

Next, insert the coppery spider chrysanthemums around the base of the arrangement and towards the top. Then add longer stems of preserved eucalyptus to form a gentle diagonal line pointing down towards the smaller saucepan. To complete the arrangement, fill the second pan with yellow spider chrysanthemums — a simple effect which enhances the main arrangement.

A salt box can serve as an unusual wall-vase, and this copper one provides a beautiful burnished setting for the reds and peachy colours of the flowers and foliage. First, place florists' foam into the salt box and prop open the lid at an interesting angle using a stem, twig or piece of wire.

Create a gentle diagonal line with preserved eucalyptus stems and follow this line with pale peach spray carnations, keeping the stems slightly shorter than the eucalyptus and in varying lengths. The two contrast beautifully. Recess a couple of carnations into the display to give depth and the impression that the flowers are bursting out.

Finally, place one orange lily in the centre to serve as the focal point. Two or three lily buds positioned close to the centre will open subsequently and add further interest and colour to the display.

Brass provides good highlights for floral displays and while not as warm as copper is an excellent foil for these pale autumn colours. This brass French chocolate pot is especially pretty with its wooden handle. Cut a deep piece of florists' foam to fit into the pot and soak it well.

Use about eight dried onion heads to create the outline, placing the tallest two first to establish the height and then adding progressively shorter ones on either side to form a dome-shaped outline. Mixing dried and fresh flowers can be very effective, but be sure to use wet florists' foam!

Next, take peach spray carnations of similar graduating heights and slot them in between the onion heads, filling in the outline. Finally, to complete the main arrangement, coral can be used to add a contrast of texture and help give substance. A strategically placed piece of coral and a carnation head lying with the lid complete the picture.

The bright red label and seal of an old-fashioned mustard jar has been cleverly picked up by the scarlet carnations. To begin the display, put a piece of soaked florists' foam into the mustard jar.

Fill the jar with carnation foliage and intersperse with red carnation buds and flowers. Offset the rather symmetrical look by creating a diagonal line with a few stems of variegated ivy.

In this attractive arrangement, gently flowing lines and contours have been created with just three varieties of flower. And the salt jar — with its 'open mouth' — provides a perfect backdrop, with both the top and the base clearly visible in the completed display. First, place a piece of soaked florists' foam into the jar.

Begin the display with several stems of delphinium. Their naturally curving stems will form a gentle outline. Recess a little bouvardia into the jar to create depth.

The central flowers are alstroemeria. Push most of them well into the centre, leaving several longer stems to protrude and strengthen the outline.

A Chinese wok and rice bowl form an unusual but effective setting. Tape soaked florists' foam to a shallow dish and place inside the wok. Position four exotic bird of paradise leaves to create a sweeping line and add a few bird of paradise flowers. Use *Leucodendron* foliage to cover any visible foam and trail some over the wok edge.

Varying lengths of yellow spider chrysanthemums help form the centre of the arrangement: keep the long stems to the back and shorter stems to the fore. Position capsicum (known as Christmas pepper in the United States) stems throughout the arrangement to form the focal point. The capsicums will also pick up the red of the bird of paradise.

Delicate *Oncidium ornithorhynchum* orchids soften the effect of the arrangement: position two or three stems to take up the sweeping line of the bird of paradise leaves. Then add the bear grass, curving it up above the arrangement to create the 'oriental' effect.

Insert a few remaining flowers into some soaked florists' foam in the small rice bowl. Keep the stems short except for a longer spray or two of *Oncidium* orchid which reflect the main arrangement.

U sing this unusual plant pot holder, three individual arrangements combine to form an attractive display. Place soaked florists' foam into each pot and then arrange the pots one at a time. Fill the first with two lengths of delphiniums, the open flowers close to the rim of the pot, the longer stems sweeping out. Among this recess clumps of *Viburnum tinus.*

In the second pot place six or seven open pinks and two or three buds. Recess with pretty September flowers (a form of aster) to add depth to the arrangement.

The third pot forms the focal point of the whole arrangement, with purple and lilac anemones looking up and out, interspersed with tiny pink carnation flowers and leaves. Allow a trail of ivy to wend its way from the saucer at the base of the pots to complete the display.

An old stoneware hot water bottle and kitchen jar make a simple but effective display when placed together. Use crushed wire mesh to hold the arrangement in the jar and position the yellow gerbera to form a gentle contour.

Take longer stems of *Oncidium ornithorhynchum* orchids, and fill in behind and around the gerbera, following the contour already established. A finger of foam inserted into the hot water bottle will take the smaller arrangement. This comprises a stem of gerbera cut short and a sprig of *Oncidium*.

In this continental-style arrangement, the different types of flowers are grouped together, rather than interspersed, to create a stunning effect on top of a simple glass cake stand. First, fix wet florists' foam to the cake stand using a plastic pin-holder.

Then, using long stems of *Liatris*, position several sprays upright at the back of the display and several more horizontally at the front, lying slightly to one side of the dish.

Group cream spray chrysanthemums to one side of the arrangement as shown, graduating their length so that the longest flower falls gently over the edge of the stand. Balance this with a stem or two on the opposite side of the arrangement to create continuity. Finally, fill in the centre and foreground with a group of lilac chrysanthemums.

T his sumptuous arrangement of plump flowers on a green glass cake stand looks almost edible! Place a round piece of soaked florists' foam in the centre of the stand. Then use yellow roses and alstroemeria alternately, cutting the stems on a slant and keeping them short so that once inserted into the foam the flower heads rest on the edge of the dish.

Finally, top the 'cake' with a few sprays of mimosa which will retain its pretty fluffy heads longer if conditioned first. This is done by submerging flower heads under cold water then dipping stems into 2.5cm (1in) of boiling water for a few seconds. Stand in a jug of warm water until the flowers have dried off.

The next layer comprises the bobbly 'flowers' of *Leucodendron brunia* followed by a ring of Persian buttercups. The latter will last longer if their stems are put into boiling water for a few seconds, before being given a long drink.

What better way of displaying a pretty dried arrangement and keeping it dust-free than under a glass cheese dome? Fix dry florists' foam to the base with a plastic pin-holder. Cover the foam with dried hydrangea heads, some of which have been previously part-sprayed with gold paint. Add some brown-dyed protea twigs and seed-heads.

To make the arrangement asymmetrical, add the orange-dyed statice on one side to form a gentle curve which sweeps down and away from the focal point — the *Helichrysum*. Keep the pretty 'faces' of the everlasting *Helichrysum* looking up and out, with the more orange-coloured ones close to the orange statice.

Complete the arrangement with two varieties of yarrow, slotting them among the hydrangea opposite the statice. The mustard-coloured yarrow not only enhances the autumnal effect of the arrangement but adds a soft texture. (Yarrow is an easy plant to preserve as it dries quickly without water.)

This beautiful Doulton cheese dish is enhanced by a mass of russets and creams and would make a striking centrepiece at a dinner party.

Fix some soaked florists' foam to a pin-holder placed in the centre of the base. Use short stems of rust coloured chrysanthemums to establish the outline of the display. Place the tallest chrysanthemum in the centre; the rest should graduate down to the shortest stems near the base.

Between the chrysanthemums insert cream spray carnations, recessing them into the arrangement. Rust-dyed *Limonium* should be used to fill in any gaps and a few trailing stems will serve to balance the display.

This arrangement makes an ideal centrepiece for any table but especially a low coffee table where the pretty faces of the anemones can be seen to their best advantage. Half fill a clear glass bowl with water. Then select 12 to 15 anemones and cut their stems down to around 2-3cm (1-1½in).

Place the anemone heads on the surface of the water and intersperse with little clumps of *Viburnum tinus* to add contrast.

A second smaller bowl looks very attractive with the main arrangement and helps to break up the symmetry of the outline. Fill a smaller bowl with large shining marbles and water. Then position just two or three anemone heads on the surface with a little sprig of gypsophilia (also known as baby's breath in the United States) so that the marbles can still be seen.

The warmth of natural wood is a perfect complement to the rich green tones of this display. First place a piece of cling film (plastic wrap) into the bowl to protect the wood from the water. Then tape a square brick of soaked florists' foam to a small saucer and place inside the salad bowl.

Arrange stems of foliage as shown, using small-leafed eucalyptus and marguerite foliage. Let the stems curve up and out from the bowl, putting in plenty to act as a solid backdrop.

Sear some stems of variegated *Euphorbia marginata* (see page 11) and slot in among the other foliage somewhat randomly. Then 'sprinkle' about eight to 10 marguerites throughout the arrangement, lifting and highlighting the whole display.

Perfect for a special cocktail party! Cut the top from a large pineapple and slice a smaller pineapple in half lengthways. Scoop out the fruit and put soaked florists' foam into both pineapples. Insert fern fronds in the larger fruit to form the outline. Create the focal point with white lilies — shorter full flowers at the front, a longer stem at the back to give height.

Complete the larger display with two stems of orange flowering *Euphorbia fulgens* and three orange tulips. Recess one tulip into the lilies. In the smaller pineapple place three additional orange tulips having cut them short so that they sit close to the foam. Add just one curving stem of flowering *Euphorbia* to the left of the display. Cocktail accessories add the finishing touch.

Make the most of unusual vegetables. Here, the centre of a squash is scooped out to create two unusual containers. Put some soaked florists' foam into both 'skins'. Form a 'pyramid' with *Choisya ternata* foliage in the main piece of squash and add a few fern fronds. From this mass of foliage extend ten to twelve tulips in contrasting colours of orange and red and yellow stripes.

Into the display recess several cream spider chrysanthemums. These come in sprays but the individual flowers on their own short 'stems' are perfect for creating depth.

Fill in the outline with seven or eight white iris. For the top of the squash use stems of 'Huckleberry' and *Choisya* foliage to form an outline and fill in with a simple mixture of cream spider and rust-coloured daisy chrysanthemums. These colours beautifully complement the main arrangement.

A golden honeydew melon makes a practical and pretty container for flowers. Cut a wedge from the melon (just under a quarter) and scoop out most of the flesh from the fruit, putting it into the refrigerator to eat later! Insert a piece of soaked florists' foam into the fruit and slot in several stems of eucalyptus to create the outline.

Position a few daffodils first, cutting their stems on a slant to make them easier to insert into the foam. Keep all but one of the daffodils to roughly the same length, placing them on one side of the arrangement. Cut the last one shorter and put it in the foreground as the focal flower. On the opposite side to the daffodils insert two long stems of jonquil.

Bring more jonquil through the front of the display and recess a couple behind the focal daffodil. Add three purple hyacinth heads next, one either side of the focal daffodil, the other at the back to the left. Complete the picture with three white double tulips.

A stylish setting such as this modern yellow speckled fruit bowl really warrants creativity. Use contrasting colours and craft clever lines to achieve the best effects. Push half a brick of florists' foam well down into the bowl. Build up the outline with the tallest flowers — white stock and blue hyacinths — intermingling them.

To create the 'V' shape, arrange the red tulips and white 'rose' tulips alternately in a diagonal line down one side of the display. Finish at the bottom with a red tulip, then work up the other side to complete the 'V'. Cover the visible foam with small pieces of lilac *Limonium* and take longer sprays around the outline, trailing a little over the rim of the bowl.

This exquisite orange glass bowl is set off magnificently with a selection of orchids. Place a piece of soaked florists' foam in the centre of the bowl and carefully surround it with marbles. This will hold the foam in position and prevent it from being seen through the glass.

Begin with a group of long-stemmed dark red *Arachnis* (scorpion) orchids, placing four or five stems to one side of the bowl and a couple at the back to establish the height of the arrangement. Put one stem lying forward over the front of the bowl. Next, position a group of pale orange and white *Dendrobium* orchids in the front of the display reserving one or two to rise up at the back.

Having filled the front of the bowl with *Dendrobium* orchids, create the focal point by adding three dark red *Cymbidium* orchids to the centre of the arrangement.

A striking red enamel coffee pot and mug form the basis for this pretty display of red anemones. Place some soaked florists' foam into the coffee pot and fill with clumps of flowering marguerite foliage.

Among the marguerite foliage slot three or four pieces of seared *Euphorbia marginata* (see page 11). Fill in this outline with graduating heights of bright red anemones, reserving three longer stems to serve as a 'spout'.

The smaller arrangement is created quickly and easily. Take a piece of soaked florists' foam, place it in the mug and fill it with the remaining clumps of marguerites.

Tea-pots are often employed as flower holders. This one — in the shape of an elephant — is a little more novel than most, but the idea can be adapted to suit any type of pot. Put a crushed piece of wire mesh into the tea-pot and add some water.

Enhance the lovely grey colour of the pot by using similar coloured foliage. Shown here is small leafed eucalyptus 'sprinkled' with gypsophilia (also known as baby's breath in the United States). This creates the basic outline of the arrangement.

Use dramatic lilac and purple anemones to create the focal point, forming an 'umbrella' over the foliage. The darker anemones also give the display depth and a velvety texture. Fill in the outline with pink miniature carnations.

The rough hessian of coffee sacks provides a good background material for this display. Put dry florists' foam into the first sack and fill out with crushed newspaper or tissue. Cover the foam with yellow and brown-dyed *Limonium,* then add grains and grasses such as wild oats, *Phalaris* and wheat. Bells of Ireland also add interest, texture and height.

Build up the design with brown plants such as Ti-tree, *Stirlingia, Leptocarpus,* dried protea and *Gynerium.*

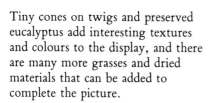

Tiny cones on twigs and preserved eucalyptus add interesting textures and colours to the display, and there are many more grasses and dried materials that can be added to complete the picture.

Another sack, similarly packed with foam and crushed paper, achieves a different effect with the addition of teasels, brown-dyed *Limonium* and *Helipterum roseum.*

W̲hen using novelty containers such as this, try to keep flowers and foliage to a minimum so that both plants and container can be fully enjoyed. Put a piece of soaked florists' foam into the jug and build up the outline with a few flowers. In this case, the pig's soft shades have been picked out with pink-edged white double tulips and white stock.

To fill out the display add longer stems of pale pink spray carnations and pink daisy chrysanthemums. Extra length and contrast can be achieved with two or three carnation leaves.

A quaint cottage tea-pot serves as an excellent vase, with the colours of the cottage picked-out by the clever choice of flowers. Begin by placing some soaked florists' foam into the teapot and insert stems of eucalyptus to form a base for the display.

Next, add four or five pink-edged white double tulips, placing the longest tulip stem in the centre of the arrangement to establish the height. Keep the tulip leaves on the stems as their texture and colour add contrast to the other flowers and foliage.

Fill in the outline with purple-dyed *Limonium*, recessing some pieces to create depth. Finally, take a few purple anemones and position them throughout the display. As the focal flowers of the display their faces should be prominent.

To preserve the singular colour of this serene arrangement, green marbles have been used in a green glass jug. Place the marbles in the jug — carefully — before adding the water. Then build up the basic outline with bear grass, allowing the blades to curve out on either side of the jug. Next, add about three bird of paradise leaves so that they curve out from the centre of the display.

Add two long stems of bells of Ireland, one slightly shorter than the other, and fill in the outline with *Leucodendron* foliage. To the front place a couple of pieces of variegated foliage — in this case *Euphorbia marginata*. This must be seared first to seal the stem (see page 11). Be careful not to get the milky substance from the stem on to the skin as it will cause irritation.

In the small glass mug place water only and fill with a clump of *Euphorbia marginata*. This offsets the larger arrangement beautifully.

P lain glass provides a most effective setting for the elegant contours of the arum lily (also known as calla lily). Fill the jar with small leafed eucalyptus, packing plenty in to hold the wide heavy stems of the arum lilies. Place a few sprays of eucalyptus at the back to establish the height and insert several arum lilies of graduating heights among the foliage, following the outline.

Fill in the outline with four shaggy-edged peach carnations and four tiny white roses. Although the carnations appear as the focal point of the display, they also serve as a sharp contrast to the arum lilies and help set both flowers off to their best advantage. A little eucalyptus and a peach carnation in the smaller jar balances the larger display.

An old candy jar has been used for the basis of this beautiful display, and the marbles, though used predominantly to hold the arrangement in position, add a pretty touch to the overall effect. Build up the outline with the mimosa, then add several stems of purple iris at varying heights as shown.

Use yellow roses to form the focal point, positioning one or two slightly off centre for balance. Add a few sprays of lemon-cream statice — longer stems at the side, shorter ones close to the rim of the jar — to provide a contrast of texture and complement the rich yellow of the mimosa and roses.

Finally, put three or four white carnations among the arrangement, recessing one or two smaller ones. These help to break up the solid mass of yellow. A little spray of mimosa, positioned on the glass stopper at the foot of the jar, adds the finishing touch.

A novel toothbrush holder and soap dish are ideal for bathroom flower displays. Beginning with the toothbrush holder, fill it with water and place a small group of *Brodiaea* to one side. Follow with a group of pink nerines in the centre, and then add more *Brodiaea*. Back the display with a little naturally dried *Limonium*.

For the soap-bearing duck use a pin-holder to secure some florists' foam to the dish. Then fill the dish with the tops of hyacinths, cutting the stems at an angle with a sharp knife as they are quite thick and otherwise unmanageable. (This is a good way of using up hyacinths once the bottom parts have started to die.)

Complete the arrangement in the soap holder with a few *Brodiaea* florets and sprigs of *Limonium*.

PINK PLUMAGE

This 'marble-effect' duck is actually made from papier maché and would, therefore, be ruined by the use of water. Consequently, an attractive display of dried plants has been arranged inside it. Place some dry florists' foam into the duck and cover with purple and white *Limonium*.

Fill in the 'plumage' with lilac-coloured *Limonium*. This plant is easily obtainable from most florists and is a useful and pretty base for many dried arrangements. *Limonium sinuatum* or statice comes in numerous 'new art shades' of salmon, orange, yellow, carmine, blue and lavender.

Complete the duck's plumage with other dried grasses such as the plump, fluffy *Lagurus* (also known as rabbit or hare's tail grass) and the feathery *Agrostis pulchella* which creates a 'tail'. Lilac ribbons inserted among the arrangement enhance the display.

An old water jug and bowl provide a perfect setting for this traditional mass arrangement, with its bold contours and colours. Wedge left-over scraps of soaked florists' foam into the jug. Then position a few large stems of bells of Ireland with two or three garlic flowerheads to establish the height and outline.

Place white statice and grey *Kochia* (summer cypress) foliage to fill in the outline, keeping the stems around 5cm (2in) shorter than the garlic and bells of Ireland. Next add scabious (known as pincushion flower in the United States) among the statice and *Kochia.* Already the colours complement the jug and bowl beautifully.

Brilliant red Persian buttercups, placed within the mass, instantly lift the arrangement, their colour and texture a striking contrast to the existing plants. To finish, place a small sprig of lacey *Viburnum tinus* inside the bowl to the fore of the jug, or, instead, more short-stemmed flowers can be added to the bowl, surrounding the jug.

Here, a rich and traditional display has been created using a wide range of varieties and colours. A vase such as this needs only water, but crushed wire mesh or florists' foam can be used. Begin by filling the jug with variegated *Pittosporum* — this will give the arrangement depth. Then intersperse a few spider chrysanthemums for contrasting texture.

On this solid base add a good mixture of flowers to develop a symmetrical display. The arrangement shown here uses mainly carnations, chrysanthemums, gerbera and scarlet tobacco plant (known as flowering tobacco in the United States) in co-ordinating colours.

The swirling design on a pretty chamber pot is picked up by the arrangement within it, an effect which can be achieved with any attractively patterned container. Begin with the yellows — Ti tree, lady's mantle, golden rod and yarrow — keeping the arrangement informal and natural. Next, add some light brown dried *Limonium* and red-headed *safflower*.

Pick up the colours from the pot's design using the red-headed *safflower*. Then add some dried brown grasses and brown seed heads, keeping the arrangement wide and full.

The most fragile plants — honesty and Chinese lanterns — should be added last. These give the arrangement body and contrasting texture as well as off-setting the glorious orangey-reds in the pattern of the pot.

The warm, earthy quality of terracotta is often used to house plants. Here, three small, plain little pots set off the different types of fresh flowers beautifully. Soaked florists' foam can be used for the larger two pots, water only for the small one. Start by arranging several anemones in the largest pot.

Add longer stems of pink broom, setting it at a rakish angle on each side. To fill in the outline use longer stemmed Persian buttercup buds. Depth and contrasting texture is provided with two stems of *Leucodendron brunia*. Recess one deep into the pot, the other longer piece towards the back.

Position three pink hyacinths of graduating lengths in the medium bowl. Fill in around the base with *L. brunia*, leaving the feathery foliage trailing over the edge. To finish, fill the small bowl with short stems of white daisy chrysanthemums.

CRÈME DE LA CRÈME

A collection of pretty milk and cream jugs are enhanced by the addition of a few flowers. Place florists' foam into the larger jugs, just water into the smaller ones. Beginning with the central jug, fill it with stems of pink orchid and a little feathery asparagus fern.

Insert taller stems of pink orchids into the jug at the back of the display and offset with white spray carnations. Take the carnations through the outline of both the back and central jugs so they create an effect of continuity.

The mauve stripe in the jug on the left is picked up by three deep purple anemones. Add to this just a few sprigs of peach-coloured flowering *Euphorbia fulgens*. The *Euphorbia* is then continued in the tiny jug in the foreground. Balance the purple anemones with a bunch of blue-dyed yarrow in the last jug.

Agroup of pretty little bottles in bright cobalt blue make an eye-catching setting for well-chosen flowers. Just put water into the bottles. Start with the tallest bottle at the back and fill with stems of delphinium and a little asparagus fern. In the bottle to the left, use shorter stems of miniature iris and yellow Persian buttercups.

In the central bottle place a small piece of *Euphorbia marginata* foliage, a stem of white stock and a single white freesia. This softens the bold primary colours picked up again by the blue-dyed yarrow in the bottle on the right. Complete the setting with two yellow Persian buttercups and a little mimosa in the smallest bottle at the front.

Picking up the Scottish theme of the pewter tankard, the deep rich reds and greens of this striking display cleverly echo a tartan design. Wedge left over scraps of soaked florists' foam into the tankard and then start the display with two bird of paradise leaves positioned at the rear.

Next, add several long stems of *Arachnis* (scorpion) orchids, fanning them out and above the bird of paradise leaves.

Pick up the red in the stripes of the orchids with a dozen dark red spray chrysanthemums cut to varying heights. These form the focal point of the arrangement and help fill in the outline. This display is long-lasting providing the foam is watered regularly.

Old beer and medicine bottles make an attractive setting for a group of flowers or foliage. Because of their tight necks, only water (if fresh flowers are used) is necessary. Start by putting a spray and a single carnation flower into the central bottle.

Then add one or two stems of freesia to two of the other bottles. Create height by putting *Dendrobium* orchids and bird of paradise into a fourth bottle, allowing the latter to soar up above the other flowers. Complete the picture with a tiny orchid bloom in the smallest bottle.

Pretty floral displays in two small but sturdy house plant containers serve as excellent book ends. Put well-soaked florists' foam into the pots. Then check that the pots are heavy enough to support the books. It would be a great pity to complete the arrangements only to find that the books knock over all your hard work and creativity!

Arrange the flowers in such a way that each display has a 'flat' side which can be put up against the books. Taking the first pot begin by filling it with sprengeri fern, creating a diagonal outline.

Follow the outline with rust-coloured spray chrysanthemums, then add the focal point using white double tulips. Use three or four tulips of differing heights, taking them through the centre of the display.

Fill in the outline with yellow Persian buttercup buds and flowers. (These will last longer if properly conditioned first: put the ends of the stems into boiling water for a few seconds before giving them a long drink.) To complete the picture, similarly arrange the flowers in the second pot, creating a 'flat' surface on the opposite side to that in the first display.

Brighten up an obsolete typewriter by using it as a background for some cheerful spring flowers. Begin by taping some soaked florists' foam onto a small saucer and placing into the 'well' of the typewriter keys. Cut the stems of a few full-blooming white lilies in graduating heights and insert into the foam. Position a lily bud to rise at the back of the display.

Next, take six yellow tulips and fill in the outline formed by the lilies. For co-ordinating colour, yet contrasting texture, recess several stems of fluffy mimosa. Note how effectively the cream and gold of the flowers are reflected in the typewriter keys.

Zany gift bags in shiny metallic colours provide an eye-catching setting. Take three bags of varying size and colour. Put one small sherry or wine glass into each of the smaller bags and two glasses in the larger bag. Put some soaked florists' foam into the glasses. Start with the pink bag and arrange graduatings stems of blue flowers: *Dendrobium* orchids, blue-dyed yarrow and grape hyacinths.

To complete the pink bag add one blue-dyed carnation. Three pale pink double tulips beautifully offset the blue of both the bag and flowers. Cut them to differing heights and position in the blue bag. Continue the blue by placing three dyed carnations in the silver bag. Crushed tissue paper, some satin ribbon and a single pink nerine completes the pictures.

An old wicker shopping basket provides an excellent setting for a long-lasting dried arrangement. Take a whole brick of florists' foam and fix to a pin-holder in the base of the basket. Disguise the foam by packing pieces of beige-dyed *Limonium* all around it and inserting natural *Limonium* into the centre.

Fill in with yellow-dried flowers — lady's mantle and golden rod — allowing some longer stems to trail over the edge of the basket. Lengthen the whole arrangement with stems of bells of Ireland, creating a long diagonal line across the length of the basket. Follow this line with brown grasses.

In the centre add some sprays of honesty; its silvery heads will lighten the solid mass of mustards and browns. Brown-dyed teasels can be added next — their spiky heads peeking out from the other plants, providing contrasting texture and complementary colour. Against these muted colours dot a sprinkling of bright mixed *Helichrysum* throughout the arrangement.

Finally, complete with some preserved beech leaves. (Preserve in advance by mixing one part glycerine to two parts hot water. Give beech stems a good drink of water first then place into the solution and leave for about 10 days, coating the leaves with a little of the mixture. Store in a box until ready to use.)

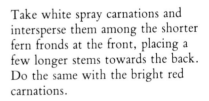

Here, a wicker waste-paper basket forms the basis of an attractive arrangement of ferns and carnations. Note how the colour of the basket has been picked out in the flowers to create a stunning effect. Begin by taping soaked florists' foam into a container and positioning it inside the basket. Then fan out the fern fronds to form the setting for the flowers.

Take white spray carnations and intersperse them among the shorter fern fronds at the front, placing a few longer stems towards the back. Do the same with the bright red carnations.

Finish off by adding a sprinkling of September flowers (a form of aster) to soften the whole effect. (This display can also be achieved by pushing tiny phials of flowers into the soil of a real fern, such an arrangement being known as a pot-et-fleurs — see page 27).

A dustpan is, perhaps, not generally considered as a container for flowers but, as this design shows, such a utensil can make an attractive setting for a low-lying arrangement of bright spring flowers. Tape some soaked florists' foam to a saucer and place in the dustpan. Cover the foam with *Choisya ternata* foliage.

Begin to create the outline with fern fronds, extending them beyond the *Choisya* foliage. Then use bright yellow daffodils of similar length to form a strong diagonal line across the display, lying parallel to the shorter line already established by the fern fronds.

Strengthen this outline with orange tulips, extending them beyond the daffodils in all directions, yet keeping the general strong diagonal line intact. Gently open one tulip in the centre to create a focal point. Fill in the outline with stems of peach coloured flowering *Euphorbia fulgens*, recessing a few stems to give depth.

There is nothing quite like a mass of flowers and, here, armfuls of pink tulips set against a black plastic basket look simply stunning. Put a heavy container into the shopping basket to weight it down, then fill the container with water. Add numerous tulips of varying shades of pink — the more flowers the better. Position them sweeping out of the basket in a fairly random fashion.

Little else is needed in this type of wanton arrangement. Just add a touch of laurel foliage as a contrast to all the tulips. Before displaying the laurel, hammer the stems first, then give them a long drink of water.

Equally stunning as the basket full of pink tulips is a bag full of black tulips — even if the flowers *are* only plastic! Tape some dry florists' foam into a heavy container to hold the arrangement in place and put into a fashion bag. Arrange the black tulips to form the outline, then fill in with more of the same.

Intersperse the black tulips with several blue-green ones to match the bag. Complete the display by filling in the gaps with bunches of green net secured on wires and inserted into the foam.

Sunny yellow provides a perfect backdrop for these bright spring yellows and lilacs. Prop open the lid of the case with a small stick and insert a brick of soaked florists' foam wrapped in cling film (plastic wrap). Begin by grouping some closely cut white iris to the right of the case, standing them upright at the back. Next to them insert a bunch of white net.

In front of the iris, group eight to ten yellow Persian buttercups and a touch of foliage. Six or seven white double tulips fill virtually the rest of the case. Retain their leaves as these add an attractive contrast of colour to the display.

On the far left of the case, and in among the tulips, slot three or four purple hyacinths. For the finishing touch add a little piece of lilac net, bunched on some wire, in the top right hand corner to balance the colour scheme.

Frothy strawberry and vanilla ice cream colours spill from this little attaché case. Begin by wrapping a brick of soaked florists' foam in cling film (plastic wrap) and fit it into the case. Form the outline with small-leafed eucalyptus; into this recess four or five white spray chrysanthemums. Position some stems of white stock to one side of the case to establish the height.

Next, gather two shades of pink net into small bunches and secure at the base with wire. Place two or three net bunches at the back of the display and one small piece at the front in the corner. Then, following the outline, put pale pink spray carnations throughout the arrangement.

For the focal point use single deep pink carnations. Trail two sprays of *Dendrobium* orchids from the two front corners of the case. Finally, fill out the outline with pink-dyed *Limonium*.

Employ the picnic hamper, before the summer comes, as a setting for groups of spring flowers. Place some soaked florists' foam on a dinner plate and fit into the hamper. Prop open the lid at a fairly wide angle with a small stick. 'Line' the basket with Portuguese laurel and begin grouping the flowers. Start with just two white lilies in the bottom right hand corner.

Next, arrange several orange tulips, in a diagonal line extending from the tip of the basket lid to the left edge of the basket handle.

Add clumps of white lilac to fill the centre of the display, removing nearly all the foliage first. (To condition the lilac, hammer the stem ends really well before giving them a long drink in warm water.)

Next, group a bunch of three or four purple iris beside the lilac, and finally add another cluster of tulips, this time yellow ones to complement the rest of the design. Complete the display with fern fronds and variegated ivy trailing from the front of the basket.

Achieve a pleasing design with a green-tinged glass goblet and just three varieties of flowers. Carefully fill the goblet with marbles before adding the water. Start by positioning three bright crimson carnations to form the heart of the display. Then build up around them using five or six more carnations.

Fill in the outline with some alstroemeria and white lilac, hanging a stem of lilac gently over the rim of the glass. Complete the display with a few Portuguese laurel leaves. Remember that any display using marbles will shift slightly as you progress, so do not aim for too formal an arrangement — rather a more free-flowing one.

Put a couple of empty Coca-Cola cans to good use by creating this stunning linear arrangement. Take the tops off two cans with an opener and smooth down any rough edges. Put soaked florists' foam into both cans. To complement the design of the can use bold red and yellow tulips. Keep one red tulip tall, then graduate the height of the other tulips.

Position a cream spider chrysanthemum close to the can and one longer stem reaching halfway up the display. Then insert a little bear grass, looping the ends back into the can. Place one single red and yellow striped tulip — with its petals gently eased backwards — into the second can and finish off with a little foliage.

This simple but effective arrangement of flowers and foliage is held in place by the tight neck of the decanter which, in turn, restricts the number of plants in the display. Begin by filling the vessel with water and positioning three wild garlic flowerheads at graduating heights.

Then add a few fern fronds as shown here, and trail a stem of variegated ivy down in front of the decanter. Finally, position the focal flowers — three cream spray chrysanthemums — putting two short ones close to the rim of the decanter with one taller one behind. The cream is the dominant colour of the arrangement, picked up in the chrysanthemums, the garlic and the ivy.

To highlight the pattern on these pretty containers, the gold of the decanter has been cleverly picked out by the choice of flowers in the display. Begin by spraying dried love in a mist seed heads with gold paint. When dry, insert a number of sprays into the vessel, varying their height to create an outline. Reserve a few for the small jug.

Add three white full carnations to form the focal point of the arrangement and complement the gold. Help fill in the outline with orchid sprays, pointing them downward towards the smaller jug which can then be filled with a few dried and sprayed love in a mist.

A DROP OF PINK BUBBLY!

An attractive pink champagne bottle is offset with matching roses and delicate blossoms of broom. Half fill the bottle with water. A narrow-necked bottle is best with thin stems of flower sprays; so place just one stem of pink broom and one of small pink roses in the bottle. Cut the rose stem at an angle and trim off excess leaves so that only the stem is in the water.

As a perfect finish to the display add some delicate bear grass, bringing a couple of the blade ends back into the neck of the bottle to create the attractive loops. In the matching champagne glass carefully position a few marbles and fill with water. Place shorter sprays of broom and roses in the glass to complete the arrangement.

This highly effective arrangement only requires a cocktail shaker and flowers of one basic colour — a creamy yellow. Put a piece of soaked florists' foam into the shaker base, then insert three gerbera flowers, graduating the length of the stems. Add just a little foliage (in this case carnation foliage) behind and in front of the second tallest gerbera.

Position some curving sprays of yellow broom on either side of the display. The spiky flowers of the broom contrast with the soft petals of the gerbera. Reserve some short stems of broom and insert into a small piece of soaked florists' foam which has been positioned in the shaker lid. Place at the base of the main arrangement.

Keep the champagne in the refrigerator and use the ice bucket for red roses! First, put soaked florists' foam at the base of the bucket. Then insert some variegated foliage — shown here is a spine-less form of holly. Intersperse this with eight or nine red roses, still in bud. Have two or three longer stems rising from the foliage to one side at the back.

Fill in all the available space with jonquil, following the outline. The gold is highlighted by the yellow-edged foliage. (A handy tip: the roses will last longer if the stems are placed in boiling water for a minute before being given a long drink.)

Ahandsome old stoneware filter jar is a handy container for flowers, but a whole brick of florists' foam is needed for the arrangement because of the jar's height. Begin with sprays of sprengeri fern, trailing some stems over the sides of the jar. In the centre and to the back add long stems of white lilac. To strengthen the outline add some white stock.

Pink stock, pink roses and pink tulips dominate the display. Just a little pink stock is needed as the main flowers are the roses and the tulips. Position these throughout the display, keeping a fairly symmetrical design. The lid of the jar propped up at the base creates the finishing touch.

Old, well-preserved toys which still hold sentimental value can be put to good use as flower holders. The flowers even hide the dents and scratches! This wooden toy train with its little carriages makes an appealing display. Begin by wrapping some soaked florists' foam in cling film (plastic wrap) and placing it into the train's carriages.

Fill the first carriage with short stems of 'Huckleberry' foliage and insert five or six closely cut daisy chrysanthemums.

Add a few orange carnations flecked with red and recess some peach-coloured flowering *Euphorbia fulgens,* remembering to sear it first (see page 11). The tiny flowers and rich foliage of the *Euphorbia* give substance and depth to the 'posy'.

In the second carriage, begin the display with a single orange tulip, gently easing back its petals to give a more open effect. Surround the tulip with more 'Huckleberry' foliage and finish off with peach-coloured flowering *Euphorbia*.

A child's toy is possibly one of the least likely containers for flowers but this yellow truck provides a novel way of setting off bright orange blooms. Place a saucer of soaked florists' foam into the truck. Cover the foam with *Choisya ternata* foliage and add some orange spray chrysanthemums, picking up the colour of the bright stripes in the toy.

Fill in the outline with orange spray carnations. Next insert the focal flowers — four or five orange tulips. Keep their stems quite long so that they stand above the dense mass of foliage and other flowers. (Tulips last longer if first conditioned in a vase of water into which has been added a teaspoonful of sugar.)

Recess some cream spider chrysanthemums into the arrangement to create depth and for contrasting texture. Finally, offset the display with bright yellow Persian buttercups liberally spread throughout the display.

Verging on the ridiculous, this amusing idea is nonetheless highly effective. Place some soaked florists' foam into two small wine glasses and slot one into each boot. Begin by placing some feathery sprengai fern into the blue boot. Strengthen this outline with a few daffodils and stems of jonquil.

Add a beautiful white iris to form the focal point of the display in the blue boot. Then position two taller iris at the back, along with two white lily buds. For contrasting texture, and to create depth and substance, add a few curving stems of white lilac.

In the red boot create the outline with blue iris and a single blue hyacinth. Then add red and yellow/red striped tulips, allowing them to break out of the outline and curve gently away to follow the foot of the boot. Recess some stems of white lilac into the display and complete with four or five bright red spray carnations, keeping them close to the heart of the arrangement.

A party or special event is a good excuse for an unusual 'thematic' display. This one might go well at a theatrical gathering — or even a wedding! Begin by putting a large brick of soaked florists' foam into a container which will fit comfortably into the hat. Fan out sprays of *Mallalika* foliage and fill in with September flowers (a form of aster).

Recess white spray chrysanthemums into the foliage and use longer stems to establish the height towards the back. Have a couple trailing over the brim of the hat alongside a few of the September flowers.

The focal point of the arrangement is poinsettia flowers which should be conditioned first by searing the stem ends with a lighted candle (see page 11). Fill in the outline and balance the display with deep red spray carnations.

Here is a novel way of utilizing a pretty straw hat which is too small or past its prime. Tape some soaked florists' foam to a saucer and place in the hat. Create a soft and spidery outline with stems of sprengeri fern. Next, take three or four stems of white stock and insert into the heart of the display, bringing just one stem forward over the brim of the hat.

Use white daisy chrysanthemums to fill in the outline and give substance to the design. (These flowers are generally good survivors when cut, but they will last even longer if the stem ends are placed into boiling water first before being left in deep water for a long drink.)

In among the chrysanthemums recess some lilac hyacinth heads to create depth and a contrasting texture. Finally, complete the display with deep purple anemones. These are the main flowers, so use plenty, spreading them evenly throughout the arrangement.

Most flower arrangements look well against a natural setting. Here, coral is used as a base for freesias and *Oncidium ornithorhynchum* orchids. Wrap a piece of soaked florists' foam in cling film (plastic wrap) and place it behind the coral. Then pass the freesia stems through the coral branches and insert into the foam.

Finally, pass longer stems of *Oncidium* orchids through the back and sides of the coral and into the foam. Only one or two flower varieties will be needed with a complex container such as coral.

A goldfish bowl is one item that many people have tucked away, judging by the average lifespan of most goldfish! Put the bowl to good use by creating a really eye-catching arrangement. Fill the bowl carefully with a mixture of shells and pebbles before adding the water.

The aim is to achieve a 'waterspray' effect with the first few flowers. Start with gypsophilia (also known as baby's breath in the United States), trailing a little over the side. Next add stems of delicate blue *Brodiaea*, following the same outline.

Peach spray carnations reflect the colour in some of the shells and only a few are needed to follow the sweeping outline already established. Dried onion heads have a lovely texture and their colour is picked up by the pebbles and shells. Place eight or so throughout the arrangement, filling in the outline.

Drift or bog wood — with its natural contours — provides an ideal setting for this unusual display. Take three pieces of flat coral and insert them into a lump of soaked florists' foam which has been wrapped in cling film (plastic wrap) and attached to the wood with wire.

Position a single gerbera bloom to sit in the centre of the display, obscuring the foam and creating a focal point. Add two stems of *Arachnis* (scorpion) orchid — one at the back, the other shorter piece lying forwards — to complete the picture.

Not exactly a horn of plenty, but a conch shell with flowers, foliage and coral spilling out to form an attractive and exotic 'marine' display. To begin, wrap some soaked florists' foam in cling film (plastic wrap) and push it into the hole of the shell. (Cling film is used to prevent fragments of foam getting lost inside the shell).

Next, add some 'flowing' foliage — this *Leucodendron* resembles seaweed and is perfect for this arrangement. The peach spray carnations match the colour on the shell. Have these peeping out, following the flowing outline created by the foliage.

For dramatic contrast intersperse some brick red carnations among the peach ones, recessing one or two. Add a contrast of texture in the form of two pieces of flat coral. To complete the arrangement, arrange two long stems of striped *Arachnis* (scorpion) orchid flowing out from the shell and strengthening the outline.

The warmth of polished wood provides a beautiful backdrop for a floral display. Here the lustrous sheen of Portuguese laurel highlights the natural shine of an old wooden artist's box. Tape soaked florists' foam to a plate before inserting into the box — this will protect the wood from any water spillage.

Prop open the box with a small stick or twig. Now create the outline with Portuguese laurel, covering the foam and filling the open box.

Bright yellow double tulips are positioned next. Cut them all to approximately the same length, on the slant so that they slot into the foam more easily. Place them throughout the display. To create depth, recess several cream spider chrysanthemums, their 'feathery' heads providing a contrast of shape and texture to the rather solid lines of the other flowers.

To complete the arrangement add the focal flowers — the white lilies. Their orangey-brown pollen enhances the wood while the yellow specks on the inside of their petals highlights the boldly-coloured tulips.

Old polished wood is a perfect backdrop for any flowers, enhancing their shape and colour. Wrap cling film (plastic wrap) around some florists' foam and place in the lower drawer. Pack the drawer with forget-me-nots and a little *Brodiaea*. To the left place a little clump of *Viburnum tinus* and a tiny spider chrysanthemum. Place a few pink miniature roses to the right.

Fill the second drawer with roses and their buds, once again using florists' foam based with cling film (plastic wrap). The main mass of pink roses should appear from the left hand side of the drawer. This forms an optical line with the roses in the bottom drawer. Complete with sprigs of forget-me-nots and *Viburnum tinus* peeping out of the top drawer.

An old fashioned set of scales provides an eye-catching setting for flowers and foliage. Position a piece of soaked florists' foam into the pan of the scales and insert several stems of *Leucodendron*. Follow the outline of the scales' weighing pan with the foliage, ensuring that the foam is virtually covered.

Create the focal point using alstroemeria. Keep the stems slightly longer than the *Leucodendron*, slotting them in between the foliage so that their 'faces' look up and out from the pan.

Recess two types of dried yarrow into the arrangement to provide depth and a contrast of texture. The yellow also complements the golden streaks in the alstroemeria. To finish, add a little spray of yarrow and an alstroemeria flower sitting alongside the weights to create continuity for the eye.

CONDITIONING CHART

An A-Z of plants and how to treat them

Alstroemeria	Cut stems and place in shallow water.
Amaryllis	Slice off the bottom of stem with a sharp knife. The hollow stem often needs help to support the heavy flower head; when arranging, a thin stick can be gently inserted into the stem.
Anemone	Cut and dip stems in 2.5cm (1in) of boiling water for a few seconds before giving a long drink.
Aster	Crush stem ends and place in 2.5cm (1in) of boiling water before giving an overnight drink.
Bird of paradise	Cut stems on a slant and give a long drink.
Campanula	Cut stems and give a deep drink for a few hours.
Carnation	Cut stems at an angle between joints and place in shallow tepid water.
Christmas rose	Prick stem along its length with a needle and place in deep water.
Chrysanthemum	Cut or crush ends of stems before giving a deep cool drink.
Cornflower	Cut stems and place in water.
Daffodil	See narcissus.
Dahlia	Cut stems and place in water. Wide-stemmed varieties need to be plugged as with delphiniums.
Delphinium	Cut stems. Turn upside down and fill stem with cold water. Plug end with a little cotton wool (cotton).
Forget-me-not	Needs little conditioning except cutting stems and giving a long drink.
Freesia	Cut stems and place in shallow cool water.
Gerbera	Cut stems on a slant and put ends in 2.5cm (1in) of boiling water for a few seconds before giving a long cool drink.
Gladiola	Cut stems and put in cool, shallow water. Remove the end buds to ensure all flowers will open.
Grape hyacinth	Cut stems and put in cool water.
Gypsophilia	Needs little conditioning, except re-cutting stem ends. Easily dried by hanging upside down.
Hyacinth	Cut stems. Then wrap a sheet of non-absorbent paper around flowers and give a long deep drink.
Iris	Cut stems on a slant and give a long drink.
Ixia	Crush stems and place in cool water; if buds are tight, put in 2.5cm (1in) of boiling water for a few minutes first.
Jonquil	See narcissus.
Lilac	Remove all foliage and hammer stems before giving a long drink in warm water.
Lily	Cut stems on a slant or split at base and give a drink in cold water.
Lily-of-the-valley	Garden varieties simply need stems cutting and a drink. Forced ones need stems cutting, wrapping in tissue paper and placing in warm water. They can then be left for several hours completely submerged in cool water before arranging.
Love in a mist	Cut stems and put in water.

Marigold	Cut stems and give a deep drink in cool water.
Mimosa	Immerse the heads in cold water before dipping the stems into 2.5cm (1in) of boiling water for a few seconds. Stand in some warm water until the flowers have dried off.
Narcissus	Cut stems and put in cool, shallow water. Generally, keep daffodils apart from other plants, at least for the first 24 hours, as they produce a poisonous substance which can kill other flowers.
Nerine	Cut stems on a slant before giving a long drink.
Orchid	Generally, orchids last well in water. Cut their stems on a slant and give a long drink. Re-cut stems every few days.
Peony	Cut ends and give a long drink of warm water.
Persian buttercup	Cut and dip stem ends in boiling water before giving a long drink.
Poinsettia	Sear the end of the stem with a flame until it goes black.
Poppy	This needs searing as for the poinsettia.
Primrose	Needs stems cutting and placing in water.
Protea	Hammer the ends before giving a long drink.
Pyrethrum	These last well as cut flowers and simply need their stems re-cut before beinggiven a long drink.
Rose	Crush the ends of florists' roses before giving a long drink in warm water. Roses from the garden need their stems placed in boiling water for about a minute before being given a long drink. Roses can be revived with an aspirin tablet or a teaspoonful of sugar.
Scabious	Cut the ends of the stems and give a long, overnight drink.
Snapdragon	Cut stems and give a long deep drink for an hour or so. Forced blooms need a few seconds with their stems in 2.5cm (1in) of boiling water first.
Snowdrop	Cut stems and place in bunches in a little cool water.
Stock	Hammer stem ends and remove all foliage below the water line before giving a long drink.
Sweet pea	Trim stem ends and place in deep water in a cool place. Handle as little as possible.
Sweet william	Cut stems and give a long drink.
Trollius	Cut and dip stem ends into boiling water, then give a deep drink of cool water.
Tulip	Cut stems and wrap flowers in stiff, non-absorbent paper for a couple of hours to strengthen and straighten them. Place in shallow water. Tulips also like a little aspirin.
Violet	Place the flower heads upside down in tepid water for 30 minutes and then reverse, cut stems and place the stems into cool shallow water.
Zinnia	These hollow stems need to be cut and given a long drink. Provide a little support with a thin piece of coated wire inserted into the stem if it is especially fragile.

SCIENTIFIC CLASSIFICATION

The following is an alphabetical list of the common names of plants used in this book and their Latin equivalents.

common name	Latin name	common name	Latin name
Alstroemeria (also called Peruvian lily)	*Alstroemeria*	Honesty (or silver dollar plant)	*Lunnaria annua*
Amaryllis	*Hippeastrum aulicum*	Huckleberry	*Gaylussacia*
Anemone	*Anemone*	Hyacinth	*Hyacinthus*
Arum lily (also called calla lily)	*Zantedeschia aethiopica*	Hydrangea	*Hydrangea*
		Iris	*Iris*
		Ivy	*Hedera*
Asparagus fern	*Asparagus plumosis*	Jonquil	*Narcissus*
Bells of Ireland	*Molucella laevis*	Lady's mantle	*Alchemilla*
Bird of paradise	*Strelitzia reginae*	Lilac	*Syringa*
Bouvardia	*Bouvardia*	Lily	*Lilium*
Broom	*Genista*	Love in a mist	*Nigella*
Capsicum (also called Christmas pepper)	*Capsicum*	Marguerite	*Chrysanthemum*
		Mimosa	*Acacia*
Carnation	*Dianthus*	Mock orange blossom	*Philadelphus*
Chinese lantern	*Physalis*	Nerine	*Nerine*
Chrysanthemum	*Chrysanthemum*	Onion	*Allium cepa*
Daffodil	*Narcissus*	Persian buttercup	*Ranunculus asiaticus*
Delphinium	*Delphinium*	Poinsettia	*Euphorbia pulcherrima*
Dumb cane	*Dieffenbachia*	Poppy	*Papaver*
Eucalyptus	*Eucalyptus*	Portuguese laurel	*Prunus lusitanica*
Fern (Boston fern unless otherwise specified)	*Nephrolepis exaltata*	Rose	*Rosa*
		Safflower	*Carthamus tinctorius*
Forget-me-not	*Myosotis sylvatica*	Scabious (also called pincushion flower)	*Scabiosa*
Forsythia	*Forsythia*		
Freesia	*Freesia*	September flower	*Aster ericoides*
Garlic	*Allium sativum*	Snapdragon	*Antirrhinum*
Gerbera	*Gerbera*	Sprengeri fern	*Asparagus sprengeri*
Gladiola	*Gladiolus*	Statice	*Limonium sinuatum*
Golden rod	*Solidago*	Teasel	*Dipsacus fullonum*
Grape hyacinth	*Muscari*	Tobacco plant	*Nicotiana*
Gypsophilia (also called baby's breath)	*Gypsophilia*	Tulip	*Tulipa*
		Wheat	*Triticum*
Heather	*Erica*	Wild oats	*Arena fatua*
Holly	*Ilex aquifolium*	Yarrow	*Achillea*

INDEX

A

A Drop of Pink Bubbly! **106**
A La Mode **66**
A Winter's Day **37**
Abundance **96**
Acacia (see Mimosa)
Achillea (see Yarrow)
Agrostis pulchella **79**
Alchemilla (see Lady's mantle)
Ali Baba **64**
Allium (see Garlic, Onion)
Alstroemeria **21, 38, 42, 51, 57, 102, 123**
  conditioning **124**
Amaryllis **24**
  conditioning **124**
Amethyst **51**
Anemone **36, 42, 54, 60 68, 69, 73, 83, 84, 115**
  conditioning **124**
Antirrhinum (see Snapdragon)
Art Nouveau **21**
Arum lily **75**
Asparagus fern **84, 85**
Aster (see also September flower)
  conditioning **124**
Aucuba japonica **13**
Autumn Morning **47**
Avant Garde **97**

B

Ballet Lesson **99**
Bathtime Fun **78**
Bear grass **53, 74, 103, 106**
Beech **93**

  conditioning **12**
  preserving **93**
Bells of Ireland **28, 70, 74, 80, 92**
Bird of paradise **52, 78, 86, 87**
  conditioning **124**
Bonsai **39**
Bottled Blooms **87**
Bouvardia **51**
Box **13**
  conditioning **12**
Bright and Shiny **32**
Brodiaea **7, 117, 122**
Broom **22, 34, 41, 83, 106, 107**
Bun moss **38, 39**
Burnished Copper **46**
Buying flowers **8-9**

C

Calla lily (see Arum lily)
Camellia **13**
  conditioning **12**
Campanula
  conditioning **124**
Capsicum **31, 52**
Carnation **26, 31, 32, 38, 39, 41, 47, 48, 49, 50, 54, 59, 69, 72, 75, 77, 81, 84, 87, 91, 94, 99, 102, 105, 107, 111, 112, 113, 114, 117, 119**
  buying **8**
  conditioning **24**
Cassoulet **40-41**
Champagne and Roses **108**
Chinese lantern **82**
Chocolate Time **49**

Choisya ternata 13, 45, 64, 95, 112
Christmas rose
  conditioning 124
Chrysanthemum 18, 20, 21, 23, 26, 28, 30,
  31, 33, 34, 35, 37, 40, 43, 44, 46, 47, 52,
  59, 64, 72, 81, 83, 86, 89, 99, 103, 104,
  110, 112, 114, 115, 121, 122
  buying 8
  conditioning 10, 124
Cobalt Blue 85
Coffee Sacks 70-71
Coffee Time 68
Colour wheel 17
Conditioning 8, 10, 11, 124-125
  foliage 12
Continental, The 56
Coral 35, 49, 116, 118, 119
Coral Island 116
Cornflower
  conditioning 124
Cornucopia 119
Country Cottage 73
Country Kitchen 34
Creme de la Creme 84
Cupressocyparis 13
Cupressus
  conditioning 12
Cytisus scoparius 13

D
Daffodil 65, 95, 113
  conditioning 124
Dahlia
  conditioning 11, 124
Delphinium 26, 28, 51, 54, 85
  conditioning 11, 124
Design 16-17
Dianthus (see Carnation)
Doulton Delight 59
Dumb cane 27

E
Easter Bonnet 115
Equipment 14-15
Eucalyptus 20, 28, 32, 35, 46, 47, 48, 61, 65,
  69, 71, 73, 75, 99
  conditioning 12
Euonymus europaeus 13
Euphorbia fulgens 45, 63, 84, 95, 111
Euphorbia marginata 26, 61, 68, 74, 85
  conditioning 11
Exuberance 28-29

F
Fern (Boston) 63, 64, 94, 95, 101, 104
  (see also Asparagus, Sprengeri)
Festive Garland 44
Fire and Ice 31
Floating Anemones 60
Floral Confection 76-77
Floral Dome 58
Floral Fan 23
Flower Basket 92-93
Flowering Fern 94
Forget-me-not 33, 122
  conditioning 124
Forsythia 13, 23, 34, 39
  conditioning 10
Freesia 18, 34, 85, 87, 116
  buying 9
  conditioning 11, 124
Fruit and Flowers 65

G
Garlic 80, 104
Gateau 57
Gaultheria shallon 13
Genista (see Broom)
Gerbera 28, 55, 81, 107, 118
  conditioning 124
Gift Wrap 91
Gladiola 20, 28, 38
  buying 8
  conditioning 11, 124

Glazed Stoneware 55
Gloriana 81
Goblet 102
Gold and Silver 18
Golden Glass 105
Golden Glow 35
Golden rod 82, 92
Grape hyacinth 91
  conditioning 124
Gynerium 70
Gypsophilia 19, 60, 69, 117
  conditioning 124

H
Heather
  conditioning 12
Hebe 13
Hedera (see Ivy)
Helichrysum 58, 93
Helipterum roseum 71
High Society 20
High Tec 24
Hippeastrum aulicum (see Amaryllis)
Holly 19, 108
Honesty 82, 93
Huckleberry 64, 110-111
Hyacinth 25, 65, 66, 78, 83, 98, 113, 115
  conditioning 124
Hydrangea 35, 58
  conditioning 12

I
Ikebana 118
Ilex (see Holly)
In the Balance 123
Iris 25, 64, 77, 85, 98, 101, 113
  conditioning 11, 124
Ivy 50, 54, 101, 104
  conditioning 12
Ixia
  conditioning 124

J
Japanese Garden 38
Jonquil 65, 108, 113
  conditioning 124

K
Kochia 25, 33, 80

L
Lady's mantle 82, 92
Lagarus 79
Leptocarpus 70
Leucodendron 18, 38, 39, 47, 52, 74, 119, 123
  L. brunia 47, 57, 83
Liatris 56
Lilac 21, 100, 102, 109, 113
  conditioning 10, 11, 124
Lily 19, 21, 35, 45, 46, 48, 63, 90, 100, 113, 121
  conditioning 124
Lily-of-the-valley
  conditioning 124
Limonium (see also Statice) 59, 66, 70, 71, 73,
  78, 79, 82, 92, 99
Literary Masterpiece 88-89
Locomotion 110-111
Love in a mist 105
Lunnaria annua (see Honesty)
Lustre 120-121

M
Mahonia aquifolium 13
Mallalika 33, 40, 43, 114
Marigold
  conditioning 125
Marguerite 36, 61, 68
Mechanics 14-15
Milliner's Fancy 30
Mimosa 27, 57, 77, 85, 90
  conditioning 125
Mock orange blossom
  conditioning 11
Molucella laevis (see Bells of Ireland)
Muscari (see Grape hyacinth)
Myosotis sylvatica (see Forget-me-not)

N

Narcissus (see Daffodil, Jonquil)
Nelle the Elephant 69
Nerine 25, 78, 91
  conditioning 125
New Order 95
Nicotiana (see Tobacco Plant)
Nigella (see Love in a mist)
November Salad 61

O

Old Stoneware 109
Onion 49, 117
Orchid 84, 87, 105
  Arachnis 30, 43, 67, 86, 118, 119
  buying 9
  conditioning 125
  Cymbidium 67
  Dendrobium 20, 67, 87, 91, 99
  Oncidium 23, 53, 55, 116
Orchid Rhapsody 67
Oriental, The 52-53

PQ

Peach and Crimson Pocket 48
Peaches and Cream 75
Peony
  conditioning 125
Persian buttercup 57, 80, 83, 85, 89, 98, 112
  conditioning 125
Pestle and Mortar 33
Pig in Pink 72
Pina Colada 107
Pink on Parade 22
Pink Panorama 25
Pink Plumage 79
Pinks 54
Phalaris 70
Pittosporum 19, 81
  conditioning 12
Pockets Full of Posies 122
Poinsettia 114
  conditioning 125
Pop Art 103
Poppy
  conditioning 11, 125
Portuguese laurel 45, 100, 102, 120
Pot-et-Fleurs 27
Preservatives 10, 12
Primaries 19
Primrose
  conditioning 125
Protea 58, 70
  conditioning 125
Prunus lusitanica (see Portuguese laurel)
Pyrethrum
  conditioning 125

R

Ranunculus asiaticus (see Persian buttercup)
Re-conditioning 12
Red Label 50
Rhododendron
  conditioning 10, 12
Rich Velvet 80
Rose 18, 20, 42, 43, 57, 75, 77, 106, 108, 109, 122
  buying 9
  conditioning 10, 125
Royal Flush 36
Ruscus 30
  conditioning 12

S

Safflower 82
Scabious 25, 80
  conditioning 125
Scotland the Brave 86
Searing 11
Seascape 117
Secretary 90
September flower 28, 36, 54, 94, 114
Shrubs to grow at home 13
Simplicity 104
Singapore Sling 62-63
Singing in the Rain 113
Skimmia japonica 13
Snapdragon 30
  conditioning 125
Snowdrop
  conditioning 125
Solidago (see Golden rod)
Splendour 26
Sprengeri fern 21, 88, 109, 113, 115
Spring Picnic 100-101
Spring Sunshine 98
Statice 26, 58, 77, 80
Stem structure 10-11
Stirlingia 70
Stock 42, 66, 72, 85, 99, 109, 115
  buying 9
  conditioning 10, 125
Strelitzia reginae (see Bird of paradise)
Sugar and Spice 42
Summer cypress (see Kochia)
Sweet pea
  conditioning 125
Sweet william
  conditioning 125
Syringa (see Lilac)

T

Teak 45
Teasel 71, 93
Terracotta Collection 83
Terracotta Trio 54
Ti-tree 70, 82
Tobacco plant 81
Top Hat 114
Tough Truck 112
Tranquility 74
Trollius
  conditioning 125
Tulip 42, 45, 63, 64, 65, 66, 72, 73, 89, 90, 91, 95, 96, 97, 98, 100, 103, 109, 111, 112, 113, 121
  conditioning 11, 125

UVW

Vermillion 43
Viburnum tinus 31, 32, 34, 37, 38, 39, 54, 60, 80, 122
  conditioning 11
Victoriana 82
Violet
  conditioning 11, 125
Wheat 70
Wild oats 70

XYZ

Yarrow 26, 44, 58, 82, 84, 85, 91, 123
Zinna
  conditioning 125

ACKNOWLEDGEMENTS

The publishers wish to thank the following for their help in compiling this book:
Coca-Cola Great Britain, Pemberton House, Wrights Lane, London W8
The Covent Garden General Store, Long Acre, London WC2
David Mellor, St James Street, London WC2
Table Props Hire Ltd, Duncan Terrace, London N1